For my children,
may you never stop blooming...

Library of Congress Control Number: 2019904292

ISBN 978-1-7327376-1-7 (HC)

All photographs by Heather Blume

Printed and bound in the United States of America

First Printing, June 2019

Published by Blume's Taxonomy LLC
P.O. Box 1892
Eagle, ID 83616

www.blumestaxonomy.com

ABC VEGGIES

Heather Blume

MS, RD, LD, SNS

A is for **asparagus,** a spear of sparrow grass.

1

B is for **broccoli**, a brainy bunch, first-in-class.

2

C is for **carrot**, an orange snack to crunch.

D is for **dill,** to digest and eat for lunch.

E is for **escarole**, an easy leaf to eat.

F is for **fennel,** a fat bulb that is sweet.

G is for **garlic**, a great clove to savor.

H

is for **h**orseradish, with a hot, spicy flavor.

I is for **iceberg lettuce**, a crispy leaf to see.

9

J is for **Jerusalem artichoke,** just as tall as can be.

K is for **k**ale, a key leaf to eat.

L is for leek, a long sheaf to heat.

M is for **mushroom,** to munch on for lunch.

N is for **Napa Cabbage**, a leafy green with a crunch.

O is for **onion,** one healthy food.

P is for **p**arsley, an herb that tastes good.

Q is for **quinoa,** quite a seed to toast.

R is for **r**adish, a rad root to roast.

S is for **spinach,** a super green sight.

T is for **turnip,** to turn into a bite.

U is for **upland cress**, to pick up and chew.

V is for **vine leaf,** which very few use.

W is for **watermelon radish,** a wacky, rare treat.

X is for **xiphophyllous aloe vera,** an extra sharp plant to eat.

Y is for **yam,** a yummy orange root.

Z is for **zucchini,** a zesty squash, also a fruit.

VEGETABLE INDEX

ASPARAGUS (uh-spAIR-uhguhs)

A firm stalk that grows in the ground. Eat it raw in salads or roasted, grilled, or stir-fried with other vegetables. While harmless, a compound in asparagus may make urine smell different for some people.

BROCCOLI (brAHk-uh-lee)

A dark green plant related to cabbage. Eat the stalk and the large flowering head as a vegetable. May be eaten raw, steamed, roasted, or shredded into salad.

CARROT (kAIR-uht)

An orange, purple, or cream-colored root that grows to a point. Wash, and eat raw or steam, bake, or cook for a softer consistency.

DILL (dIl)

An herb in the parsley family, with delicate green leaves and yellow flowers. The leaves and seeds of dill are used for flavoring a variety of dishes. Dill may be eaten raw or cooked, or added to salads or sauces.

ESCAROLE (Es-kuhr-rohl)

A plant related to endive with slightly bitter leaves. Try it sautéed, cooked into soups, or chopped fresh in salads.

VEGETABLE INDEX

FENNEL (fEn-l)

A plant with yellow flowers, feathery leaves, and a white bulb. Any part of the plant may be eaten. While the leaves, or fronds, may be eaten raw in salads, the stalks and bulb may be sautéed or cooked into soups.

GARLIC (gAHR-lik)

A bulb that is often divided into sections called cloves. Garlic cloves may be eaten raw or cooked. When cooked, the cloves' pungent, spicy flavor mellows and sweetens. The green tops, or scapes, have a milder flavor and may also be eaten.

HORSERADISH (hORs-rad-ish)

A root vegetable used as a spice and processed into a condiment. May be eaten raw, which provides the strongest flavor, or pickled, or cooked.

ICEBERG LETTUCE (IEs-buhrg lEt-uhs)

Grows into a dense round head of crisp, pale leaves, which are often eaten in salad. Iceberg lettuce wilts when heated, losing quality.

JERUSALEM ARTICHOKE (juhr-rOO-suh-luhm AHR-tuh-chohk)

A species of sunflower, also called sunroot, sunchoke, or earth apple. May be cooked or roasted, but eating too much can cause upset stomach in some people.

28

VEGETABLE INDEX

KALE (kAYl)

A leafy green vegetable that may be eaten raw, cooked, or even baked into kale chips. Kale is a very healthy food, with lots of vitamins, minerals, and compounds that fight various diseases.

LEEK (lEEk)

A plant with long, broad leaves that is related to onions and garlic. May eat the white base of the leaves (above the roots and stem base) and the light green parts of the plant.

MUSHROOM (mUHsh-room)

The plump body of a fungus, typically produced above ground on soil or on a source of food. *Be careful to only eat varieties sold in grocery stores because wild mushrooms may be poisonous.*

NAPA CABBAGE (nAp-u kAb-ij)

A tall head of green leaves, with white veins. Leaves inside the plant are lighter in color and more yellow. May be eaten cooked, sautéed, added to soup, or eaten raw as salad.

ONION (UHn-yuhn)

A bulb shaped plant that grows underground. Usually cooked, it may also be served raw or used to make pickles or chutneys. Onions have a strong smell when chopped and contain certain chemical substances that may irritate the eyes.

VEGETABLE INDEX

PARSLEY (pAHR-slee)

A green herb that may be used both to flavor foods and as a garnish. Parsley leaves may be curly or flat. Certain types of parsley may be grown for the root, which may be eaten raw or cooked, like carrots.

QUINOA (kEEn-wah)

An annual seed-producing plant that is related to spinach. Quinoa seeds are eaten like rice and have more protein, fiber, vitamins, and minerals than grains.

RADISH (rAd-ish)

A root vegetable with a strong, peppery taste. May be eaten raw, cooked, or pickled. The leaves, flowers, pods, and seeds are also edible.

SPINACH (spIn-ich)

A very healthy, leafy green vegetable that may be eaten raw, cooked, frozen, or dehydrated.

TURNIP (tUHR-nuhp)

A white root vegetable that may be eaten in salad, or cooked as a side, and mashed like potatoes. The leaves, or "turnip greens" may be eaten raw in salads, or braised, boiled, or sautéed.

UPLAND CRESS (UHp-luhnd krEs)

A peppery leaf that is eaten raw in salads or on sandwiches, or cooked like spinach and used in casseroles or soup.

VEGETABLE INDEX

VINE LEAF (vIEn lEEf)

The leaf of a grapevine, which may be eaten raw in a salad for a tangy, citrus-like flavor. May also be wrapped around a mixture of rice, dill, mint, and lemon and cooked to make a Greek food called dolmades.

WATERMELON RADISH (wAWt-uhr-mel-uhn rAd-ish)

A firm, crisp root with a mild taste that's slightly peppery and slightly sweet. Larger than regular radishes, they may be eaten raw, cooked, or pickled.

XIPHOPHYLLOUS ALOE VERA (zih-FUH-fill-US Al-oh vAIR-uh)

A succulent plant that may be eaten with care. Only the skin and gel are edible, although some health food stores sell aloe vera juice. *Do not eat aloe vera skin care products, these are not safe for consumption.*

YAM (yAm)

An edible tuber that comes in a variety of colors. May be eaten boiled, fried, roasted, or cooked and mashed like potatoes.

ZUCCHINI (zu-kEE-nee)

Botanically classified as a fruit, it is often eaten as a vegetable. It grows on a vine in varying shades of green and yellow. May be eaten raw, cooked, sautéed, or grilled.

GARDENER'S DEFINITION

VEGETABLE:

The portion of a plant that does not contain seeds and can be eaten as food. This includes leaves, stem, roots, tubers, bulbs, and flowers.

1

Which of these vegetables

is **green?**

2

Which of these vegetables
is **different?**

3

How many **onions**

are in this picture?

4

How many bulbs of <u>garlic</u>

are in this pile?

36

What **color** is the inside

of this yam?

6

What **shape** are these watermelon radish slices?

38

Which words
rhyme?

LEEK

KALE

SNAIL

Which words
rhyme?

DILL

HERB

GRILL

sNACK IDEAS!

1 Carrot + Hummus

2 Broccoli + Ranch

3 Spinach + Craisins + Almond slices

Like **ABC Veggies?** Check out

ABC FRUIT

Learn the Alphabet with Fruit-Filled Fun!

ABC FRUIT

Heather Blume

MS, RD, LD, SNS

A is for **apple,** a sweet and crunchy treat.

B is for **banana**, a soft bite to eat.

www.ingramcontent.com/pod-product-compliance
Lightning Source LLC
Chambersburg PA
CBHW060752150426
42811CB00058B/1387